B Alan Bourgeois

PUBLISHING ISSUES AUTHORS DEAL WITH

Multi-Award-Winning-Author
B Alan Bourgeois

Publishing Issues

B Alan Bourgeois

Publishing Issues Authors Deal With

© B Alan Bourgeois 2025

All rights reserved. No part of this publication may be reproduced, stored in a retrieval system, or transmitted in any form or by any means, electronic, mechanical, photocopying, recording, or otherwise, without the prior written permission of the publisher.

The information and opinions expressed in this book are believed to be accurate and reliable, but no responsibility or liability is assumed by the publisher for any errors, omissions, or any damages caused by the use of these products, procedures, or methods presented herein.

The book is sold and distributed on an "as is" basis without warranties of any kind, either expressed or implied, including but not limited to warranties of merchantability or fitness for a particular purpose. The purchaser or reader of this book assumes complete responsibility for the use of these materials and information.

Any legal disputes arising from the use of this book shall be governed by the laws of the jurisdiction where the book was purchased, without regard to its conflict of law provisions, and shall be resolved exclusively in the courts of that jurisdiction.

ISBN: 9798348399023

Publisher: Bourgeois Media & Consulting (BourgeoisMedia.com)

Publishing Issues

B ALAN BOUERGEOIS

STORYTELLING
LITERACY & HERITAGE

Thank you for purchasing this limited edition book, offered in celebration of the author's 50-year milestone. Proceeds from your purchase support the Texas Authors Institute of History, a museum founded by the author in 2015, dedicated to preserving the legacy of Texas authors.

https://TexasAuthors.Institute

B Alan Bourgeois

Dear Fellow Authors,

I'm delighted to introduce this book—and every guide in this series—as a short, easy-to-read resource designed to help you succeed in your writing journey. As writers, our true passion lies in creating stories, and I understand that delving into the business side of publishing might not be where we wish to spend most of our time.

That's why I've made a conscious effort to keep things simple and straightforward, focusing on practical advice without unnecessary fluff. You'll find that some concepts overlap between books, and that's intentional—to reinforce key ideas and ensure that whichever guide you pick up, you're equipped with valuable tools to enhance your success.

I genuinely hope you find these guides enjoyable and helpful. Your feedback means the world to me, and I look forward to hearing about your experiences and triumphs.

Happy writing, and here's to your continued success!

Publishing Issues

Introduction

Welcome to "*Publishing Issues Authors Deal With*," a comprehensive guide designed to help authors navigate the complex and often challenging world of publishing. Whether you're a first-time writer or a seasoned author, the journey from manuscript to published book is filled with obstacles that can be daunting and discouraging. This book aims to demystify the publishing process and equip you with practical strategies to overcome the most common hurdles authors face.

The Ever-Changing Landscape of Publishing
The publishing industry is in a constant state of flux, driven by technological advancements, shifting market trends, and evolving reader preferences. As a result, authors must continuously adapt to stay relevant and succeed. Traditional publishing routes are increasingly competitive, while self-publishing offers both opportunities and challenges. Understanding the landscape is the first step toward making informed decisions about your publishing journey.

Why This Book Matters
Publishing a book is a significant achievement, but the road to that accomplishment is often paved with rejection, self-doubt, and logistical challenges. Many authors give up on their dreams because they lack the knowledge or resources to navigate these obstacles. "*Publishing Issues Authors Deal With*" provides you with the insights, tools, and encouragement needed to persevere.

What You Will Learn

In this book, we explore ten critical hurdles that authors commonly encounter in the publishing process. Each chapter delves into a specific issue, offering detailed explanations, real-world examples, and actionable advice. Here's a preview of what you'll find:

1. **Rejection**: Learn how to handle rejection from publishers and agents, interpret feedback constructively, and stay motivated despite setbacks.
2. **Editing**: Discover the importance of self-editing, how to choose the right professional editor, and tips for working effectively with your editor to polish your manuscript.
3. **Marketing**: Understand the essentials of building an author platform, leveraging social media, and developing a marketing plan to promote your book successfully.
4. **Distribution**: Explore the various distribution channels available to authors, including traditional and independent options, and strategies for maximizing your book's reach.
5. **Finding an Audience**: Identify your target audience, engage with readers, and build a loyal following through effective communication and community-building techniques.
6. **Time Management**: Learn how to balance writing with other commitments, set realistic goals, and use productivity tools to stay on track.
7. **Cost**: Get insights into budgeting for your book, cost-saving tips, and funding options to manage the financial aspects of publishing.
8. **Self-Doubt**: Overcome self-doubt and imposter syndrome with strategies for building confidence, seeking support, and maintaining motivation.
9. **Legal Issues**: Understand the legalities of publishing, including copyright, plagiarism, and defamation, to protect your work and avoid legal pitfalls.
10. **Formatting**: Master the technical aspects of formatting your book for print and digital platforms, ensuring a

Publishing Issues

professional presentation that enhances the reader experience.

A Roadmap to Success
Each chapter is designed to provide you with a roadmap to navigate the specific hurdle it addresses. You'll find practical advice backed by real-life examples and expert insights, giving you the confidence to tackle each challenge head-on. Whether you're struggling with the emotional toll of rejection, the complexities of editing, or the intricacies of marketing and distribution, this book offers solutions that are both realistic and achievable.

Empowering Authors
"*Publishing Issues Authors Deal With*" is more than just a guide; it's a companion on your publishing journey. By the end of this book, you'll have a deeper understanding of the publishing process and the tools to overcome the challenges that stand in your way. Our goal is to empower you to turn your manuscript into a published work and to share your stories with the world.

Thank you for embarking on this journey with us. Let's navigate the path to publishing success together.

B Alan Bourgeois

Chapters

1. Rejection — 10
2. Editing — 14
3. Marketing — 16
4. Distribution — 19
5. Finding an Audience — 21
6. Time Management — 23
7. Cost — 25
8. Self-Doubt — 27
9. Legal Issues — 29
10. Formatting — 31

About the Author — 33
Other Books by the Author in this Series — 34

Publishing Issues

1
Rejection

Aspiring writers dream of the day when they can finally see their work in print, but the path to publication is often riddled with rejection. Whether it's from publishers or literary agents, receiving a rejection letter can be a crushing blow to a writer's confidence and motivation. However, it's essential to remember that rejection is part of the writing process and doesn't mean the end of the road. Here are some tips on how writers can overcome the challenge of rejection and stay motivated in their pursuit of publication.

Understanding the Numbers

Rejection is a common experience for writers. Publishers and literary agents receive thousands of submissions each year, and the competition is fierce. According to various industry statistics, the acceptance rate for unsolicited manuscripts can be as low as 1-2%. Understanding these numbers can help put rejection into perspective. It's not a personal indictment of your abilities but rather a reflection of the highly competitive nature of the publishing industry.

Learning from Feedback

When a rejection comes with feedback, it can be a valuable learning opportunity. Instead of viewing it as a critique of your talent, consider it constructive criticism. For example, if an agent mentions that your plot is intriguing but your characters need more development, take this as a cue to work on character depth in your next draft. By learning from feedback, you can improve your writing and increase your chances of acceptance in the future.

Resilience Strategies
Developing resilience is crucial in the face of rejection. Here are a few strategies:
1. **Keep Writing**: Rejection can be demoralizing, but it's crucial to keep writing. Use it as an opportunity to improve your craft, explore new topics, and develop your voice. Don't let the fear of rejection paralyze you from pursuing your passion.
2. **Develop a Thick Skin**: Rejection is part of the publishing industry, and it's essential to develop a thick skin. Don't take it personally. Instead, use it as a learning opportunity to improve your writing.
3. **Celebrate Small Successes**: Celebrate the small successes along the way, such as positive feedback from beta readers or a request for a full manuscript. Staying motivated through these small victories is essential to maintain momentum.

Researching Publishers and Agents
Before submitting your work, do your research on publishers and agents who specialize in your genre. This increases the chances of your work being noticed and finding the right fit for your book. Here are some steps to take:
1. **Identify Potential Matches**: Use resources like Writer's Market, QueryTracker, and Manuscript Wish List to find agents and publishers who are looking for books in your genre.
2. **Read Submission Guidelines Carefully**: Each publisher and agent will have specific submission guidelines. Following these guidelines meticulously shows professionalism and increases the likelihood of your manuscript being considered.
3. **Tailor Your Submission**: Customize your query letter and submission to align with the preferences and

Publishing Issues

requirements of each publisher or agent. A personalized approach can make a significant difference.

Revising and Editing

Before you even think about submitting your manuscript, ensure it is polished and well-written. Here's how:
1. **Self-Editing**: Take the time to revise and edit your work. This process involves checking for plot holes, refining character development, and ensuring consistency throughout the manuscript.
2. **Seeking Feedback**: Get feedback from trusted beta readers or writing groups. They can provide fresh perspectives and identify areas for improvement that you might have missed.
3. **Professional Editing**: Consider hiring a professional editor if your budget allows. A professional editor can provide an objective review and polish your manuscript to a high standard.

Networking

Building relationships with other writers and industry professionals can provide valuable support, feedback, and advice. Here are some ways to network:
1. **Attend Writing Conferences**: Writing conferences are excellent opportunities to meet agents, publishers, and fellow writers. They often offer workshops, pitch sessions, and networking events.
2. **Join Writing Groups**: Being part of a writing group can provide a support system where you can share experiences, exchange critiques, and gain insights into the industry.
3. **Engage on Social Media**: Platforms like Twitter, LinkedIn, and Facebook have vibrant writing communities. Engaging with these communities can lead to valuable connections and opportunities.

Considering Self-Publishing
If traditional publishing isn't working out, self-publishing is a viable option. Here's what you need to know:
1. **Maintaining Creative Control**: Self-publishing allows you to retain full creative control over your book, from the cover design to the final content.
2. **Marketing and Distribution**: While you'll need to handle marketing and distribution yourself, there are many tools and platforms available to help, such as Amazon Kindle Direct Publishing, IngramSpark, and social media marketing.
3. **Financial Considerations**: Self-publishing can be costly upfront, but it also offers potentially higher royalties and the ability to control pricing.

Staying Persistent
Perseverance is key in the writing industry. Keep submitting your work and don't give up on your dream of publication. Here are some tips:
1. **Set Realistic Goals**: Break down your larger goals into smaller, manageable tasks. This approach can make the path to publication seem less daunting.
2. **Stay Organized**: Keep track of your submissions, feedback, and deadlines. Organization helps you stay on top of the process and reduces stress.
3. **Seek Inspiration**: Read success stories of authors who faced numerous rejections before achieving success. Knowing that others have faced and overcome similar challenges can be incredibly motivating.

Rejection is a common challenge writers face when pursuing publication, but it's important to remember that it's not the end of the road. Keep writing, revise and edit, network, and consider self-publishing as an alternative to traditional publishing. Develop a thick skin and celebrate small successes along the way. With perseverance and hard work, writers can overcome the challenge of rejection and achieve their publishing goals.

Publishing Issues

2
Editing

Editing is a critical phase in the writing process that ensures your manuscript is polished, coherent, and engaging. Many writers struggle with editing, often finding it more challenging than the actual writing. Whether you choose to self-edit, seek feedback from beta readers, or hire professional editors, the goal is to refine your work to its highest potential.

Self-Editing Tips
Self-editing is the first step in the editing process. Here are some strategies to help you effectively self-edit your manuscript:
1. **Take a Break**: After completing your manuscript, take a break before starting the editing process. This will give you a fresh perspective when you return to your work.
2. **Read Aloud**: Reading your manuscript aloud can help you catch awkward sentences, repetition, and errors that you might miss when reading silently.
3. **Focus on One Element at a Time**: Instead of trying to catch everything in one pass, focus on one element at a time, such as grammar, dialogue, or pacing.
4. **Use Editing Tools**: Utilize editing tools like Grammarly, ProWritingAid, and Hemingway to catch grammar and style issues. However, don't rely solely on these tools; they are supplements, not replacements for thorough editing.

Choosing the Right Editor
Professional editing can make a significant difference in the quality of your manuscript. Here's how to choose the right editor:

1. **Types of Editors**: Understand the different types of editors:
    - **Developmental Editors**: Focus on the overall structure, plot, and character development.
    - **Copy Editors**: Concentrate on sentence structure, grammar, and style.
    - **Line Editors**: Pay attention to the flow, clarity, and readability of each sentence.
    - **Proofreaders**: Check for final errors in spelling, punctuation, and formatting.
2. **Finding an Editor**: Look for editors who specialize in your genre. You can find editors through professional associations, recommendations from other writers, or platforms like Reedsy and Editage.
3. **Sample Edits**: Request a sample edit to see if the editor's style and feedback align with your needs. This also gives you an idea of the editor's approach and professionalism.

Working with an Editor
Building a collaborative relationship with your editor is essential. Here's how to work effectively with an editor:
1. **Clear Communication**: Discuss your expectations, goals, and any specific concerns with your editor before they start working on your manuscript.
2. **Be Open to Feedback**: Accept constructive criticism with an open mind. Remember, the editor's goal is to help you improve your manuscript.
3. **Ask Questions**: If you don't understand a suggestion or disagree with a change, ask for clarification. Editing is a collaborative process, and open communication is key.

Editing is an essential part of the writing process that can significantly enhance the quality of your manuscript. By effectively self-editing, choosing the right professional editor, and building a collaborative relationship, you can ensure your book is polished and ready for publication.

Publishing Issues

3
Marketing

Once a book is published, marketing is crucial to ensure it reaches a broad audience. However, marketing can be challenging for writers who may not have experience in this area. Effective marketing involves building an author platform, leveraging social media, and developing a comprehensive marketing plan.

Building a Platform
An author platform is your presence as an author, both online and offline. Here's how to build a strong platform:
1. **Website and Blog**: Create a professional website and consider starting a blog. Your website serves as the central hub for your author presence and a place where readers can learn more about you and your work.
2. **Email List**: Building an email list is one of the most effective ways to engage with your readers. Offer a freebie (like a short story or sample chapter) to encourage sign-ups.
3. **Public Speaking**: Engage in public speaking opportunities, such as book signings, readings, and literary events. This helps you connect with potential readers in person.

Social Media Strategies
Social media is a powerful tool for book promotion. Here's how to use it effectively:
1. **Choose the Right Platforms**: Focus on platforms where your target audience is most active. Popular choices include Facebook, Twitter, Instagram, and LinkedIn.

2. **Consistent Branding**: Maintain a consistent brand across all your social media profiles. This includes using the same profile picture, bio, and posting style.
3. **Engage with Your Audience**: Regularly interact with your followers by responding to comments, participating in discussions, and sharing valuable content. Engagement helps build a loyal reader base.
4. **Content Planning**: Plan your content in advance. Mix promotional posts with engaging content such as writing tips, behind-the-scenes looks, and personal anecdotes.

Traditional vs. Digital Marketing

Balancing traditional and digital marketing methods can maximize your book's reach. Here's how to approach both:
1. **Traditional Marketing**: This includes book signings, press releases, print advertisements, and sending copies to reviewers. Traditional marketing can help establish credibility and reach a local audience.
2. **Digital Marketing**: This involves online ads, social media campaigns, email marketing, and virtual book tours. Digital marketing can reach a global audience and is often more cost-effective than traditional methods.

Developing a Marketing Plan

A comprehensive marketing plan outlines your strategies and goals. Here's how to develop one:
1. **Define Your Goals**: Clearly define what you want to achieve with your marketing efforts. This could include increasing book sales, growing your email list, or building your social media following.
2. **Identify Your Target Audience**: Understand who your readers are and where they spend their time. This will help you tailor your marketing efforts to reach them effectively.
3. **Budget**: Allocate a budget for your marketing activities. This includes costs for ads, promotional materials, and professional services.

Publishing Issues

4. **Timeline**: Create a timeline for your marketing activities, starting well before your book's release date and continuing post-launch.

Marketing is a crucial aspect of a book's success. By building a strong author platform, leveraging social media, balancing traditional and digital marketing methods, and developing a comprehensive marketing plan, you can ensure your book reaches a broad audience and achieves its full potential.

4
Distribution

Distribution can be a significant challenge for independent authors who do not have access to traditional publishing channels. Understanding the various distribution options and strategies is essential for ensuring your book reaches readers.

Understanding Distribution Channels
There are two main types of distribution channels: traditional and independent. Here's an overview:
1. **Traditional Distribution**: Traditional publishers typically handle distribution through established networks, including bookstores, libraries, and online retailers. This route provides broad reach but is often difficult for new authors to access.
2. **Independent Distribution**: Independent authors can distribute their books through platforms like Amazon Kindle Direct Publishing, IngramSpark, and Smashwords. These platforms offer various tools and services to help authors manage their distribution.

Print vs. Ebook Distribution
Both print and ebook formats have their own distribution challenges and strategies. Here's how to navigate each:
1. **Print Distribution**:
    - **Print-on-Demand (POD)**: POD services like CreateSpace and IngramSpark allow you to print books as orders come in, reducing upfront costs and inventory management issues.
    - **Bookstores and Libraries**: Getting your book into bookstores and libraries often requires a distributor or wholesaler. Research local

Publishing Issues

   independent bookstores and library acquisition processes.
2. **Ebook Distribution**:
   - **Major Retailers**: Distribute your ebook through major retailers like Amazon Kindle, Apple Books, Kobo, and Google Play. Each platform has its own submission guidelines and royalty structures.
   - **Aggregators**: Use aggregators like Draft2Digital or Smashwords to distribute your ebook to multiple retailers and libraries from a single platform.

Global Reach

Expanding your book's distribution to international markets can significantly increase your readership. Here are some tips:
1. **International Retailers**: Ensure your book is available on international platforms. Amazon, Apple Books, and Kobo have global reach.
2. **Translations**: Consider translating your book into other languages to reach non-English speaking readers. You can hire professional translators or use translation services.
3. **Regional Marketing**: Tailor your marketing efforts to different regions. Understand local reading preferences and cultural nuances to effectively promote your book.

Distribution is a crucial aspect of getting your book into the hands of readers. By understanding the different distribution channels, navigating print and ebook distribution, and expanding your reach to international markets, you can ensure your book has the best chance of success.

5
Finding an Audience

Writers may struggle to find an audience for their work, particularly in a crowded market with many competing books. Identifying and engaging with your target audience is essential for your book's success.

Identifying Your Target Audience
Understanding who your readers are is the first step in finding your audience. Here's how to identify your target audience:
1. **Genre and Demographics**: Consider the genre of your book and the typical demographics of readers within that genre. For example, young adult fiction might target teenagers, while historical romance might appeal to older adults.
2. **Reader Personas**: Create detailed reader personas that describe your ideal readers, including their interests, reading habits, and challenges.
3. **Market Research**: Conduct market research to understand current trends, popular books, and reader preferences in your genre.

Engagement Tactics
Building and maintaining a loyal readership requires consistent engagement. Here are some tactics:
1. **Social Media**: Use social media platforms to interact with your audience. Share updates, host Q&A sessions, and participate in relevant groups and discussions.
2. **Email Newsletters**: Regularly communicate with your readers through email newsletters. Share exclusive content, behind-the-scenes looks, and updates on your writing progress.

Publishing Issues

3. **Reader Feedback**: Encourage readers to leave reviews and provide feedback. Engage with their comments and show appreciation for their support.
4. **Book Clubs and Reading Groups**: Participate in book clubs and reading groups. These communities are often enthusiastic about discovering and discussing new books.

Leveraging Reviews and Word of Mouth
Positive reviews and word of mouth can significantly boost your book's visibility. Here's how to leverage them:
1. **Request Reviews**: Reach out to book bloggers, influencers, and reviewers in your genre. Provide them with a free copy in exchange for an honest review.
2. **Engage with Reviewers**: Respond to reviews, thanking readers for their feedback. This interaction can build a positive relationship and encourage more reviews.
3. **Encourage Word of Mouth**: Offer incentives for readers to share your book with others. This could include referral programs, contests, or exclusive content for those who recommend your book.

Finding an audience for your book is crucial for its success. By identifying your target audience, engaging with readers, and leveraging reviews and word of mouth, you can build a loyal readership and ensure your book reaches its full potential.

6
Time Management

Writing and publishing a book can be a time-consuming process, and writers may struggle to balance their writing with other commitments. Effective time management is essential for achieving your publishing goals.

Setting Realistic Goals
Setting realistic goals helps you stay focused and motivated. Here's how to set achievable writing goals:
1. **Break Down Tasks**: Divide the writing and publishing process into smaller, manageable tasks. This makes the overall project less overwhelming.
2. **Set Deadlines**: Establish deadlines for each task. Be realistic about how much time you can dedicate to writing each day or week.
3. **Track Progress**: Use tools like spreadsheets, calendars, or project management apps to track your progress and stay on schedule.

Balancing Writing with Life
Balancing writing with other responsibilities can be challenging. Here are some strategies:
1. **Create a Writing Routine**: Establish a regular writing routine that fits into your daily schedule. Consistency is key to making progress.
2. **Prioritize Tasks**: Prioritize your writing tasks alongside other commitments. Use time-blocking techniques to allocate dedicated time for writing.
3. **Set Boundaries**: Set boundaries with family and friends to ensure uninterrupted writing time. Communicate your writing goals and the importance of having focused writing sessions.

Publishing Issues

Productivity Tools
There are various tools and methods to enhance writing productivity. Here are some recommendations:
1. **Writing Software**: Use writing software like Scrivener, Microsoft Word, or Google Docs to organize and draft your manuscript.
2. **Time Management Apps**: Apps like Todoist, Trello, and Asana can help you manage tasks and stay organized.
3. **Focus Techniques**: Techniques like the Pomodoro Technique (working in short, focused intervals) can improve concentration and productivity.

Time management is crucial for successfully writing and publishing a book. By setting realistic goals, balancing writing with other commitments, and using productivity tools, you can stay organized and make steady progress toward your publishing goals.

7
Cost

Publishing a book can be expensive, particularly if a writer hires professional editors, cover designers, and other professionals. Understanding the costs involved and finding ways to manage them is essential for a successful publishing experience.

Budgeting for Your Book
Creating a budget for your book helps you plan and manage expenses. Here's how to create a comprehensive budget:
1. **Identify Costs**: List all potential costs, including editing, cover design, formatting, marketing, and distribution.
2. **Allocate Funds**: Determine how much you can afford to spend on each aspect of the publishing process. Allocate funds based on your priorities and the importance of each element.
3. **Track Expenses**: Keep track of all expenses to ensure you stay within your budget. Use budgeting tools or spreadsheets to monitor spending.

Cost-Saving Tips
There are ways to save money without compromising quality. Here are some cost-saving tips:
1. **Self-Editing and Formatting**: If you have the skills, consider self-editing and formatting your book. This can save money on professional services.
2. **Freelance Services**: Hire freelancers for specific tasks instead of full-service providers. Platforms like Upwork and Fiverr offer affordable freelance services for editing, design, and marketing.
3. **DIY Marketing**: Learn basic marketing skills and handle some promotional activities yourself. This can reduce the need for costly marketing services.

Publishing Issues

Funding Options
Exploring funding options can help you manage the costs of publishing. Here are some options:
1. **Grants and Fellowships**: Research grants and fellowships available to writers. These can provide financial support for your writing and publishing projects.
2. **Crowdfunding**: Platforms like Kickstarter and Indiegogo allow you to raise funds from supporters. Create a compelling campaign to attract backers.
3. **Author Collaborations**: Partner with other authors for joint marketing efforts. Sharing costs and resources can reduce individual expenses.

Managing the costs of publishing is crucial for a successful book launch. By creating a budget, finding cost-saving opportunities, and exploring funding options, you can ensure your book is published without financial strain.

8
Self-Doubt

Many writers experience self-doubt and imposter syndrome, which can make it difficult to persevere with the publishing process. Overcoming these feelings is essential for maintaining confidence and motivation.

Overcoming Imposter Syndrome
Imposter syndrome can make you feel like a fraud, even when you have achieved success. Here's how to overcome it:
1. **Acknowledge Your Achievements**: Keep a record of your accomplishments and positive feedback. Reviewing these can help counter feelings of inadequacy.
2. **Set Realistic Expectations**: Understand that every writer faces challenges and setbacks. Setting realistic expectations can help you avoid feeling like a failure.
3. **Seek Support**: Talk to other writers about your feelings. Knowing that others experience similar doubts can be reassuring.

Building Confidence
Building self-confidence is crucial for overcoming self-doubt. Here are some strategies:
1. **Continuous Learning**: Invest in your writing skills through workshops, courses, and reading. The more you learn, the more confident you will become in your abilities.
2. **Positive Affirmations**: Use positive affirmations to boost your confidence. Remind yourself of your strengths and accomplishments.
3. **Celebrate Successes**: Celebrate every milestone, no matter how small. Recognizing your progress can help build confidence over time.

Publishing Issues

Support Systems
Having a support system can make a significant difference. Here's how to build and utilize one:
1. **Writing Groups**: Join writing groups where you can share experiences and receive constructive feedback.
2. **Mentorship**: Seek out mentors who can provide guidance and encouragement. A mentor's experience and perspective can be invaluable.
3. **Professional Networks**: Build a professional network of writers, editors, and industry professionals. Networking can provide opportunities for collaboration and support.

Overcoming self-doubt is essential for maintaining motivation and confidence in your writing journey. By addressing imposter syndrome, building confidence, and utilizing support systems, you can navigate the challenges of self-doubt and continue to pursue your publishing goals.

9
Legal Issues

Writers need to be aware of legal issues such as copyright infringement, plagiarism, and defamation. Understanding these legalities is crucial for protecting your work and avoiding legal pitfalls.

Copyright Basics
Copyright protects your work from unauthorized use. Here's what you need to know:
1. **What is Copyright?**: Copyright gives the creator of an original work exclusive rights to its use and distribution. This includes literary, artistic, and musical works.
2. **How to Copyright Your Work**: In most countries, copyright is automatically granted upon creation. However, registering your work with a copyright office provides legal proof of ownership.
3. **Duration of Copyright**: Copyright typically lasts for the author's lifetime plus 70 years. After this period, the work enters the public domain.

Avoiding Plagiarism
Plagiarism is using someone else's work without proper attribution. Here's how to avoid it:
1. **Cite Sources**: Always cite your sources when using quotes, ideas, or research from other works. Use a consistent citation style (e.g., APA, MLA).
2. **Paraphrasing**: When paraphrasing, ensure the rephrased content is sufficiently different from the original and includes proper attribution.
3. **Original Content**: Strive to create original content. If you're inspired by another work, add your unique perspective and voice.

Publishing Issues

Navigating Defamation Laws
Defamation involves making false statements that harm someone's reputation. Here's what writers need to know:
1. **Types of Defamation**: There are two types: libel (written defamation) and slander (spoken defamation).
2. **Avoiding Defamation**: Avoid making untrue or unfounded statements about individuals. Ensure your content is factual and supported by evidence.
3. **Legal Defense**: Truth is a defense against defamation claims. If your statements are true and can be substantiated, you are typically protected.

Understanding legal issues is crucial for protecting your work and avoiding legal problems. By being aware of copyright basics, avoiding plagiarism, and navigating defamation laws, you can ensure your writing is legally sound and protected.

10
Formatting

Formatting can be challenging, particularly when publishing ebooks that need to be compatible with different devices and software. Proper formatting ensures your book looks professional and is easy to read.

Formatting for Print
Print formatting involves preparing your manuscript for physical publication. Here's how to format your print book:
1. **Page Layout**: Set the page size, margins, and line spacing according to your printer's specifications. Common sizes include 5"x8", 6"x9", and 8.5"x11".
2. **Font and Typography**: Choose a readable font (e.g., Times New Roman, Garamond) and maintain consistent font size and style throughout the manuscript.
3. **Headers and Footers**: Include headers with the book title and author name, and footers with page numbers. Ensure these elements are consistent.
4. **Front and Back Matter**: Properly format the front matter (title page, copyright page, table of contents) and back matter (acknowledgments, author bio, index).

Ebook Formatting
Ebook formatting ensures your book is compatible with various devices and platforms. Here's how to format your ebook:
1. **File Formats**: Common ebook formats include EPUB and MOBI. Each platform may have specific format requirements.
2. **Responsive Design**: Ensure your ebook is responsive, meaning it adjusts to different screen sizes and orientations. Use reflowable text rather than fixed layouts.

Publishing Issues

3. **Interactive Elements**: Include interactive elements such as hyperlinks, bookmarks, and table of contents for easy navigation.
4. **Testing**: Test your ebook on different devices and platforms to ensure compatibility and a positive reading experience.

Tools and Resources

Various tools and resources can assist with formatting. Here are some recommendations:
1. **Software**: Use software like Adobe InDesign for print formatting and Vellum or Scrivener for ebook formatting.
2. **Guides and Tutorials**: Utilize online guides and tutorials for step-by-step instructions on formatting. Many platforms offer detailed formatting guidelines.
3. **Professional Services**: If formatting is overwhelming, consider hiring a professional formatter. This ensures your book meets industry standards.

Proper formatting is essential for a professional-looking book. By understanding the requirements for print and ebook formatting, using the right tools, and following best practices, you can ensure your book is well-presented and reader-friendly.

B Alan Bourgeois

About the Author

B Alan Bourgeois began his writing journey at age 12, crafting screenplays for *Adam-12* as an outlet to develop his style. While he never submitted these works, the experience fueled his passion for storytelling. After following the conventional advice of pursuing a stable career, Bourgeois rediscovered his love for writing in 1989 through a community college class, leading to his first published short story. Since then, he has written over 48 short stories, published more than 10 books, including the award-winning *Extinguishing the Light*, and made his mark in the publishing world.

Recognizing the challenges authors face, Bourgeois founded Creative House Press in the early 2000s, publishing 60 books by other authors in five years and gaining insights into the industry's marketing needs. In 2011, he launched the Texas Authors Association, which grew to include two nonprofits promoting Texas writers and literacy. He also created innovative programs like the Lone Star Festival and short story contests for students, and in 2016, the Authors Marketing Event, offering a groundbreaking Certification program for book marketing expertise.

Despite setbacks during the COVID-19 pandemic, Bourgeois adapted by launching the Authors School of Business, providing essential tools for authors to succeed as "Authorpreneurs." As publishing evolves, he has explored NFTs as a potential revenue stream for writers. With decades of experience, Bourgeois remains a driving force in the literary community, committed to helping authors thrive in a changing industry.

Bourgeois is currently the director of the Texas Authors Museum & Institute of History, based in Austin, Texas

Publishing Issues

Other Books by the Author in this Series

Y'all Write: A Month-Long Guide to Achieving Your Writing Goals

Unlock your creative potential with *Y'all Write: A Month of Writing Celebration and Growth*! This guide offers tips, motivation, and tools to help writers of all levels set goals, build momentum, and embrace the joy of storytelling.

Author's Roadmap to Success: Proven Strategies for Thriving in Publishing

Unlock the secrets to literary success with *Author's Roadmap to Success: Proven Strategies for Thriving in Publishing*. This essential guide provides actionable strategies to help writers build strong habits, master self-publishing, and thrive in their writing careers.

The Writer's Self-Care Guide: Top Ten Steps to Balance and Thrive

Transform your writing journey with *The Writer's Self-Care Guide: Top Ten Steps to Balance and Thrive*. This practical guide offers actionable steps to nurture your creativity, set boundaries, and achieve a balanced, fulfilling writing life.

B Alan Bourgeois

Top Ten Keys for Successful Writing and Productivity

Unlock your writing potential with *Top Ten Keys for Successful Writing and Productivity*. This guide offers actionable strategies to build consistent habits, manage time effectively, and produce high-quality work to elevate your writing

Mastering Research: Top Ten Steps to Research Like a Pro

Elevate your writing with *Mastering Research: Top Ten Steps to Research Like a Pro*. This essential guide provides practical tools and techniques to conduct thorough, credible research and seamlessly integrate it into your work.

Character Chronicles: Crafting Depth and Consistency in Creative Projects

Bring your characters to life with *Character Chronicles: Crafting Depth and Consistency in Creative Projects*. This essential guide reveals professional techniques to develop authentic, complex characters that resonate across any creative medium.

Editing Essentials: Your Guide to Finding the Perfect Editor

Transform your manuscript with *Editing Essentials: Your Guide to Finding the Perfect Editor*. This guide provides practical steps to identify, evaluate, and collaborate with the ideal editor to elevate your writing.

Publishing Issues

AI Programs Apps Authors Should Use

Revolutionize your writing with *Top Ten AI Programs Authors Should Use*. This guide explores powerful AI tools like Grammarly and Scrivener, offering practical tips to enhance creativity, productivity, and efficiency.

The Business of Writing

Master the publishing world with *Unlocking the Business of Writing*. This essential guide provides expert advice and practical tips to build your author platform, maximize royalties, and turn your passion into a thriving career.

Creating an Effective Book Cover

Create a book cover that captivates readers with *Top Ten Keys to Creating an Effective Book Cover*. This guide offers expert tips and practical advice on design, branding, and marketing to make your book stand out.

Mastering the Art of the Sales Pitch

Master the art of the sales pitch with *Mastering the Art of the Sales Pitch*. This guide provides essential strategies to captivate your audience, highlight your book's value, and drive its success.

B Alan Bourgeois

Publishing Issues Authors Deal With

Overcome publishing challenges with *Publishing Issues Authors Deal With*. This guide offers practical strategies and expert insights to help you navigate rejection, editing, marketing, and more to achieve your publishing dreams.

The Indie Author Advantage: Mastering Control, Royalties, and Reach for Self-Publishing Success

Thrive as an indie author with *The Indie Author Advantage: Mastering Control, Royalties, and Reach for Self-Publishing Success*. This guide offers actionable strategies to retain creative control, maximize royalties, and reach a global audience.

Mastering Amazon Publishing: A Comprehensive Guide to Success for Indie Authors

Achieve self-publishing success with *Mastering Amazon Publishing: A Comprehensive Guide to Success for Indie Authors*. This guide provides proven strategies to navigate KDP, boost visibility, and maximize earnings for your books.

Publishing Issues

Marketing Essentials for Authors: Proven Strategies to Boost Book Sales

Boost your book sales with *Top Ten Marketing Essentials for Authors: Proven Strategies to Promote Your Book*. This guide combines traditional and digital marketing tactics to help authors effectively connect with readers and turn their books into bestsellers.

Marketing Mastery: Avoiding Common Mistakes for Authors

Master book marketing with *Marketing Mastery: Avoiding Common Mistakes for Authors*. This guide offers actionable advice to help authors connect with readers, build a strong online presence, and achieve their publishing goals.

The Author Branding Blueprint

Elevate your writing career with *Author Brand Mastery: A Comprehensive Guide to Building and Sustaining Your Unique Identity*. This guide provides practical steps to define your brand, build a professional presence, and connect meaningfully with your audience.

B Alan Bourgeois

Reader Magnet: Top Strategies for Building an Engaged Reader Community

Build a loyal reader community with *Reader Magnet: Top Strategies for Building an Engaged Reader Community*. This guide offers actionable strategies to connect with readers, create exclusive content, and turn your audience into passionate advocates.

Author Platform Mastery: A Comprehensive Guide to Building, Monetizing, and Growing Your Audience

Build your literary empire with *Author Platform Mastery: A Comprehensive Guide to Building, Monetizing, and Growing Your Audience*. This essential guide offers practical strategies to define your brand, engage readers, and expand your reach.

Networking Success for Authors: Essential Strategies Guide

Achieve your literary goals with *Networking Success for Authors: Essential Strategies Guide*. This practical roadmap offers strategies to build meaningful connections, promote your work, and create a supportive community for lasting success.

Publishing Issues

Write, Publish, Market: The Ultimate Handbook for Author Success
ISBN:

Master the modern publishing landscape with *Write, Publish, Market: The Ultimate Handbook for Author Success*. This guide provides actionable strategies to build your author brand, attract readers, and achieve long-term success in your writing career.

Mastering Interviews: Essential Tips for Authors' Success

Excel in interviews with *Mastering Interviews: Essential Tips for Authors' Success*. This guide offers practical advice to confidently promote your work, connect with audiences, and turn every interview into a memorable success.

Mastering Event Presentations: Avoiding Common Author Mistakes

Captivate your audience with *Mastering Event Presentations: Avoiding Common Author Mistakes*. This guide offers practical strategies to avoid pitfalls, engage your audience, and deliver impactful presentations that boost your confidence and connect with readers.

B Alan Bourgeois

Survival Strategies for Indie Authors: Overcoming Challenges and Achieving Success

Thrive as an indie author with *Survival Strategies for Indie Authors: Overcoming Challenges and Achieving Success*. This guide provides practical advice and actionable tips to overcome obstacles, enhance your skills, and achieve your publishing goals.

Empowering Authors: Top Ten Strategies for Writing Success and Career Growth

Achieve your writing dreams with *Empowering Authors: Top Ten Strategies for Writing Success and Career Growth*. This guide offers practical advice and proven strategies to build habits, refine your craft, and grow your author career with confidence.

The Sacred Connection

Infuse your writing with mindfulness and purpose through *Creating with Spirit: The Sacred Art of Writing and Publishing*. This guide transforms your creative journey into a spiritual practice, empowering you to inspire readers and overcome challenges with authenticity and intention.

Publishing Issues

Beyond the Basics: Advanced Strategies for Indie Author Success
ISBN:
Elevate your indie publishing career with *Beyond the Basics: Advanced Strategies for Indie Author Success*. This guide offers actionable tips and strategies to diversify income, engage readers, and build a sustainable, thriving career.

The AI Author: Embracing the Future of Fiction

Embrace the future of storytelling with *The AI Author: Balancing Efficiency and Creativity in Fiction Writing*. This guide helps authors harness AI to boost productivity and creativity while preserving the emotional depth and artistry of creating.

The Non-Fiction Nexus: Balancing AI and Human Insight in the Future of Writing

Elevate your non-fiction writing with *The Non-Fiction Nexus: Balancing AI and Human Insight in the Future of Writing*. This guide shows how to harness AI's efficiency while preserving the creativity and ethical judgment that make your work truly impactful.

B Alan Bourgeois

Authorship Reimagined: NFTs and Blockchain Essentials
ISBN:
Embrace the future of publishing with *NFT and Blockchain Essentials for Authors' Success*. This guide explains how blockchain and NFTs can protect your work, automate royalties, and expand your audience while maximizing revenue.

Adapting Success: Your Book's Journey to Film

Turn your book into a cinematic sensation with *From Page to Screen: A Step-by-Step Guide to Adapting Your Book into a Blockbuster Film*. This guide provides practical advice and industry insights to help you navigate the adaptation process and bring your story to life on the big screen.

Beyond the Basics: Advanced Strategies for Indie Author Success
Elevate your indie publishing career with this ultimate guide to mastering advanced strategies in writing, marketing, and global distribution. Packed with actionable tips and real-world examples, it empowers authors to balance creativity with entrepreneurship and build sustainable, thriving careers.

Publishing Issues

2026: The Ultimate Year for Indie Authors

Make 2026 your breakthrough year with *The Ultimate Year for Indie Authors*. This guide offers practical strategies to optimize publishing, leverage social media, and achieve unparalleled success in your indie author journey.